Goat Math...

a **TRUE** story

Written By: Alice Clarkson

Illustrated By: Shelby Kittinger

Goat Math...

a TRUE story

This book is dedicated to...

First and foremost, I want to Thank God. To him goes all the glory.
This story doesn't happen without my hopes and dreams being in line with his.

I pray that motivates you to chase your dreams.

Next my family...

Dad....your legacy of loving nature and animals lives on with the first sweet book. I am a shepherdess because of the legacy of love for stewardship that I witnessed from childhood.

From my grandparents to my parents there was always time outside in the dirt.
I am forever grateful for the love of nature and books that was passed on to me.
To my husband Rich and to our children, thank you for always believing I could....
No matter what I said I wanted to do....no matter how crazy, not one of you suggested I stop.

There wouldn't be a Rowandale Therapy Goats without your support and constant love.

There will be enough goat's milk for your food,
for the food of your house,
and to nourish your young women.

Proverbs 27:27 CSB

Dad.......

love you more..............

ONE

goat

1

TWO

Goats

Goats need friends just like people do!

They can become sad if they are all alone...

2

3

THREE

goats...

4

FOUR

This seems like a lot of goats,
more than we had before,

So, Shepardess looks around
and thinks

WHY not more?

FIVE Goats...

6
SIX
goats...

**"Oh Pheobe,
could that be you?**

**Well of course it is,
I can hear you chew!"**

This goat has a name,
and that name is Kevin!

If we count him,
we made it all the way to

SEVEN!

8

EIGHT Goats...

NINE Goats...

9

I started counting,
but I had to start again,

look around and see,
there may actually be...

TEN

10

11 ELEVEN Goats...

TWELVE Goats...

12

THIRTEEN Goats...

Is this the most goats you have ever seen?
I simply can't believe it, I count thirteen!

13

14 FOURTEEN

Goats...

15 FIFTEEN Goats...

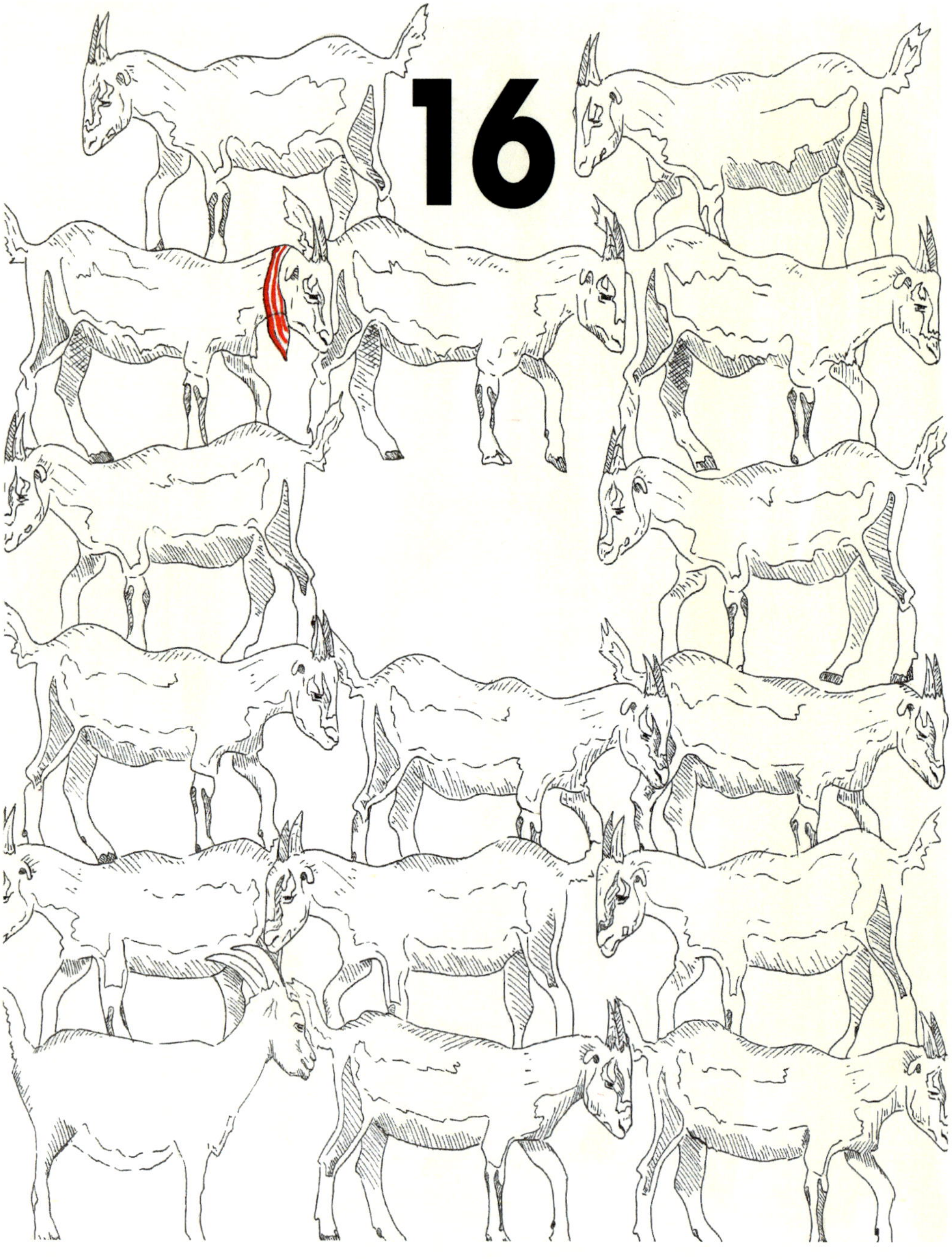
16

These goats are getting hard to count!
It was easier when there were only seven!

Has anyone seen Kevin?
He has a red scarf on, he should be easy to see,
That little goat is a mischief maker!
Maybe he's behind a tree...

17

SEVENTEEN
Goats...

EIGHTEEN

Goats...

18

NINETEEN

Goats...

19

Let's count together, we seem to have plenty

then turn the page, and see if there is 20

1
2
3
4
5
6
7
8
9
10

11
12
13
15
14
16
17
18
19
.....KEVIN

Rowandale therapy goats is a small farm in Colden, NY

These Goats are real and you can even visit them!

They are raised as therapy animals to help adults and children with special needs!

Every time you read this book you are helping them!

Thank you for being a part of their story!

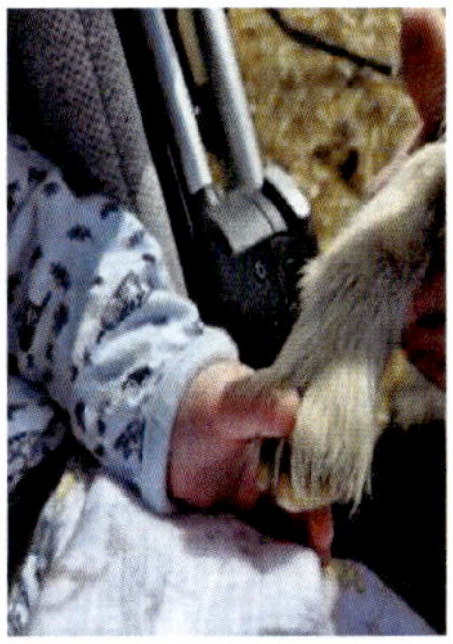

Minnie
Pheobe
Paisley
Clark
Micah
Ellie
Daisy
Miso
Winnie
Misty
Annie
Nova
Sadie
Ozzie
Bea
Esther
Mocha
Koda
Martha
Agnes

We are the Rowandale Therapy Goats!!

Author: Alice Clarkson

Alice is a Farmer and Artisan from Western New York state.
She raises and trains therapy goats on her small farm which brings visitors year-round to spend time with these gentle fun-loving animals.

Her passion and purpose is to reach people through her herd and let them see what being a shepherd feels like.

This is her first book.
The goat in this picture is sweet Martha.

Illustrator: Shelby Kittinger

Shelby is an illustrator who works with gouache and felt pen illustrations.
She loves to create worlds with detailed images that play with color.

She began illustrating books when her son was three and wishes to make books that will be loved for years to come.

Made in United States
North Haven, CT
30 August 2024

56778347R00015